Alphabet Activities

K

Written by **Hanna Otero**

Illustrations by **Creston Ely**

FlashKids
An imprint of Sterling Children's Books

This book belongs to

_____

FLASH KIDS, STERLING, and the distinctive Sterling logo are registered trademarks of
Sterling Publishing Co., Inc.

Published by Sterling Publishing Co., Inc.
387 Park Avenue South, New York, NY 10016
Text and illustrations © 2006 by Flash Kids
Distributed in Canada by Sterling Publishing
c/o Canadian Manda Group, 165 Dufferin Street
Toronto, Ontario, Canada M6K 3H6
Distributed in the United Kingdom by GMC Distribution Services
Castle Place, 166 High Street, Lewes, East Sussex, England BN7 1XU
Distributed in Australia by Capricorn Link (Australia) Pty. Ltd.
P.O. Box 704, Windsor, NSW 2756, Australia

Sterling ISBN 978-1-4114-3439-4

Manufactured in China

Lot #:
2 4 6 8 10 9 7 5 3 1
06/10

For information about custom editions, special sales, premium and
corporate purchases, please contact Sterling Special Sales
Department at 800-805-5489 or specialsales@sterlingpublishing.com.

Cover design and production by Mada Design, Inc.

Dear Parent,

Learning the alphabet is an important first step on the road to reading. *Alphabet Activities* will help your child identify letters and sounds. This book includes matching activities, hidden pictures, and lots of practice with tracing and writing letters. To get the most from *Alphabet Activities*, follow these simple steps:

- Find a comfortable place where you and your child can work quietly together.
- Encourage your child to go at his or her own pace.
- Help your child sound out the letters and identify the pictures.
- Offer lots of praise and support.
- Let your child reward his or her work with the included stickers.
- Most of all, remember that learning should be fun! Take time to color the pictures, laugh at the funny characters, and enjoy this special time spent together.

Aa

Airplane

Practice writing the uppercase letter **A**.

A

A is All Around

Circle the things in the picture that begin with the **Aa** sound.

Aa

Practice writing the lowercase letter **a**.

B b

Bike

Practice writing the uppercase letter **B**.

B

A Bunch of Balls Bb

Color the balls that show the letter **B** or **b**.

Practice writing the lowercase letter **b**.

C c

Cat

Practice writing the uppercase letter **C**.

Cool Car!

Find the hidden picture. Color the spaces that show **C** or **c**.

Cc

Practice writing the lowercase letter **c**.

Dd

Dog

Practice writing the uppercase letter **D**.

D

D Is Dandy!

Dd

Color the things that begin with the **Dd** sound.

Practice writing the lowercase letter **d**.

Ee

Elephant

Practice writing the uppercase letter **E**.

Eggs Everywhere! Ee

Color the eggs that show **E** or **e**.

Practice writing the lowercase letter **e**.

Ff

Flowers

Practice writing the uppercase letter **F**.

Frogs and Fish

Ff

Circle the things in the picture that start with the **Ff** sound.

Practice writing the lowercase letter **f**.

G g

Goat

Practice writing the uppercase letter **G**.

Great Grapes

Gg

Find the hidden picture. Color the spaces that show **G** or **g**.

Practice writing the lowercase letter **g**.

Hh

Hat

Practice writing the uppercase letter **H**.

H

Happy Horses

Hh

Color the horses wearing the **H** or **h**.

Practice writing the lowercase letter **h**.

I i

Ice Cream

Practice writing the uppercase letter **I**.

I

Icy Igloo

I i

Find the hidden picture. Color the spaces that show **I** or **i**.

Practice writing the lowercase letter **i**.

J j

Jelly Beans

Practice writing the uppercase letter J.

J

Jill and the Jack-in-the-Box

J j

Circle the things in the picture that begin with the **Jj** sound.

Practice writing the lowercase letter **j**.

Kk Kangaroo

Practice writing the uppercase letter **K**.

K

Kids and Kites

Kk

Color the kites showing **k** or **k**.

Practice writing the lowercase letter **k**.

Ll

Lion

Practice writing the uppercase letter **L**.

L

A Little Light

Find the hidden picture. Color the spaces that show **L** or **l**.

Ll

Practice writing the lowercase letter **l**.

Mm

Monkey

Practice writing the uppercase letter **M**.

M

Many M Sounds Mm

Circle the things in the picture that begin with the **Mm** sound.

Practice writing the lowercase letter **m**.

Nn

Nest

Practice writing the uppercase letter **N**.

N - - - - - - - - - - - - -

N Is Nice!

Nn

Color the things that begin with the **Nn** sound.

Practice writing the lowercase letter **n**.

Oo

Ostrich

Practice writing the uppercase letter **O**.

Ollie the Octopus Oo

Find the hidden picture. Color the spaces that show O or o.

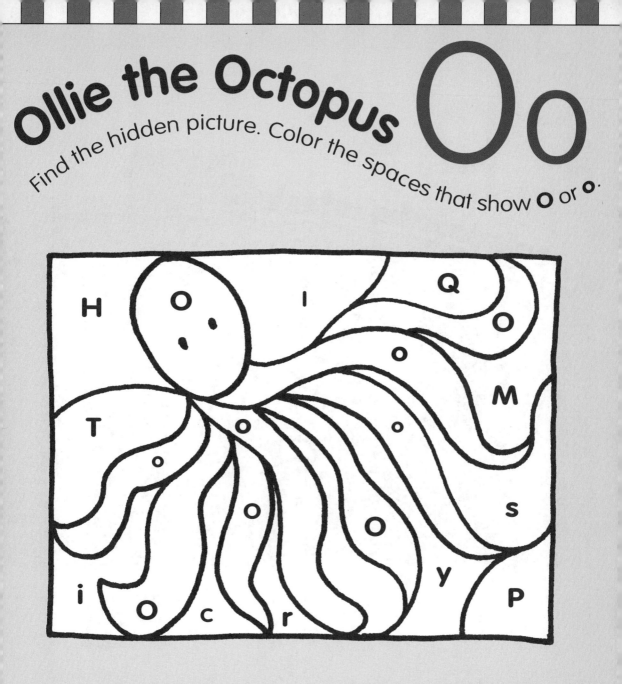

Practice writing the lowercase letter o.

P p

Pig

Practice writing the uppercase letter **P**.

P

Playful Puppies P p

Color the puppies wearing **P** or **p**.

Practice writing the lowercase letter **p**.

p

Qq Queen

Practice writing the uppercase letter **Q**.

Q Is for Quilt

Color the quilt patches that show **Q** or **q**.

Qq

Practice writing the lowercase letter **q**.

Rr

Ring

Practice writing the uppercase letter **R**.

R

Racing Rocket

Find the hidden picture. Color the spaces that show **R** or **r**.

Rr

Practice writing the lowercase letter **r**.

Ss

Sun

Practice writing the uppercase letter **S**.

S

S Is Super

Color the things that begin with the **Ss** sound.

Ss

Practice writing the lowercase letter **s**.

s

T t

Train

Practice writing the uppercase letter **T**.

Turbo Turtles

Color the turtles wearing **T** or **t**.

Tt

Practice writing the lowercase letter **t**.

U u Umpire

Practice writing the uppercase letter **U**.

Get under an Umbrella!

Uu

Find the hidden picture. Color the spaces that show **U** or **u**.

Practice writing the lowercase letter **u**.

u

V v

Valentine

Practice writing the uppercase letter **V**.

V

Violet's Violin

Find the hidden picture. Color the spaces that show **V** or **v**.

V v

Practice writing the lowercase letter **v**.

Ww

Walrus

Practice writing the uppercase letter **W**.

W

Where Are the W Words?

Ww

Color the things that begin with the **Ww** sound.

Practice writing the lowercase letter **w**.

w

Xx

X-ray

Practice writing the uppercase letter **X**.

X

Exciting x

Find and color the hidden uppercase **X** and lowercase **x** letters.

Xx

Practice writing the lowercase letter **x**.

x

Yy

Yarn

Practice writing the uppercase letter **Y**.

Y

yo-yo

Color the yo-yos that show **Y** or **y**.

Yy

Practice writing the lowercase letter **y**.

y

Zz Zebra

Practice writing the uppercase letter **Z**.

Z

Zoo Maze

Help the zebra find his way back to the zoo.

Zz

Practice writing the lowercase letter **z**.

z

The Alphabet

Trace the alphabet.

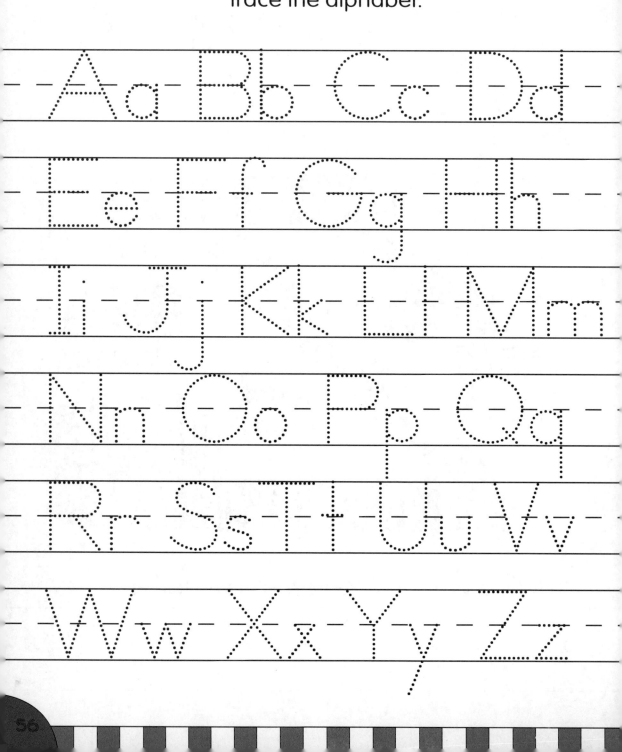

Circle the Sound

Circle the letter that shows the beginning sound.

Aa Ss Tt

Gh Hh Ii

Vv Ll Bb

Ss Dd Rr

Sounds the Same

Draw a line between things with the same beginning sound.

apple

turtle

train

star

seal

ant

Beginning Sounds

Draw a line between each picture and its beginning sound.

E e

V v

H h

B b

Make a Match

Draw a line between matching uppercase and lowercase letters.

More Beginning Sounds

Draw a line between each picture and its beginning sound.

P p

G g

J j

K k

Picture Pairs

Draw a line between things with the same beginning sound.

queen

whale

wagon

mop

monkey

quilt

Starting Sounds

Circle the letter that shows the beginning sound.

Aa Ss Cc

Rr Jj Ii

Bb Kk Ff

Tt Ii Rr

63